# CONQUER HER

TOOLS TO HELP GET YOU THROUGH THE
TOUGHER SEASONS OF LIFE

**AMANDA HERD**

# CONTENTS

Greetings v
Introduction vii

1. Tool Of Prayer 1
2. Tool Of Faith 19
3. Tool Of Consistency & Discipline 35
4. Tool Of Forgiveness 43
5. Tool Of Love 51

About the Author 59

# GREETINGS

*Conquer Her* is one of three books that will help guide you through the battlefield of overcoming yourself. *Conquer Her* was inspired by God showing me a vision of pieces to the puzzle of my life. He allowed me to see some of the greater things that He has called me to do; but in that same vision, I began to doubt myself. I was thinking that I could not successfully complete the tasks because of my past and the qualifications I believed I lacked. I watched others do some of the very things that He has called me to do, though I try my best to avoid the lane of comparison and to live outside of doubt. I had to push past all my fears and take them day by day, one step at a time, which has led me to successfully complete the task.

Although the journey continues, I am now equipped for every battle I shall come across. I desire to help those who stand where I once stood. I am here to help them get everything they need for the battle. Part one will open with all the basic tools you will need to prepare HER for the fight.

Because you are reading this book, I believe the words that are printed are PURPOSED for you. I also believe that there is much in store for you. I believe that you will finish the journey with a supernatural boldness that will help you lead all who follow you. May you read on with a receiving heart and a ready spirit. Remember this: with God on your side, you win every time, *conquer HER*.

# INTRODUCTION

Dearest Friend,

I welcome you here. Feel free to grab any of the tools that you may need from this tool bag. This bag was created JUST FOR YOU! While searching through the different compartments, you may come across a few things that may temporarily disturb you; but that's okay. I promise you I left a jewel nearby that will help you get through the process. Don't be afraid; don't be ashamed. Instead, be bold and brave. Go forth and *conquer her*!

# ONE
# TOOL OF PRAYER

Surprise, surprise! Or not. Many of us know that prayer is the key to everything in life as a believer. Learning the principles of prayer will help get you through those rough patches along the way. It is in prayer that we unlock and have access to whatever is needed. I've found numerous answers through prayer. Whether I hit rock bottom or while I stood peacefully on the hilltop, every blessing and every struggle has led me to a moment of prayer.

Taking on the challenge of capturing the culture of prayer is a beautiful process. Not saying it will be or is an easy challenge, but simply highlighting that in God's time, beauty will be revealed. Ecclesiastes 3:11 reads,

*"He has made everything beautiful in His time."*

I have found that this is a true fit even in the culture of prayer.

This tool, just like most tools, doesn't come with a standard set of instructions. We find ourselves having to figure it out. The questions come rushing in before the tool is put to trial. *How does it work? What is it? Can I do "x,y, and z" with it?* Before you know it, we find ourselves in a game of trial and error, beginning the process of capturing the culture.

Although prayer is a simple form of communication, we must understand that it is a very powerful form of impartation. When sharing and expressing our most vulnerable essence with God, we must also welcome the knowledge and wisdom of God. Many people question prayer, wanting to know what it is and how it works. In its simplest form, prayer is a conversation between you and God.

Pause and reflect on this: when you pray or desire to pray, what are you seeking? Do you look for your conversation to become visible, clear, or noticeable to your need? Do you look to grow in an area? Do you need to be heard from a distance? All of this and more are stemmed from the tool of prayer.

This tool does not only provide you with a map of personalized directions, but it also provides you with a map of redirection when you find yourself getting off course. It is in those very moments that we will need impartation the most.

In order to successfully travel throughout this journey, communication is one of the most vital tools we must use. Think of it this way: whenever we travel somewhere, especially places that we have never been before, we first look for directions. Whether we use a GPS, get Google tips or landmarks from someone who has been there before, or even simply read road signs, we look for some sort of direction which is given through communication.

Likewise, on this journey, we will find ourselves in places that we have never been before. We will find ourselves revisiting places that we've journeyed through for quite some time, and we may even find ourselves lost in a place of familiarity. In order to get ourselves back on track, we will need clarity in our direction, which will force us to use the tool of prayer.

Life's journey cannot be taken alone. We can physically be alone, but we are never alone in spirit. Simply put, we are never abandoned, even when we seem to feel alone.

We must understand the value of impartation through prayer so that we can navigate to our purposed place at our appointed time. Following God's knowledge and wisdom will always align us with the plans He has for us, at the time He desires to reveal them in the world.

Getting off track or drifting away is common. At some point, we all will find ourselves in this boat one way or another. The question is, how do we get out? Most times, when we are caught in a boat that's drifting, we feel cast aside and alone. Although many can see us, our minds are fooled by believing they can't. Though some can hear us, we are conditioned to believe they can't. Therefore, we must gain an understanding of the intent of effective communication through the tool of prayer.

Prayer can be a very tricky tool. Not only do you have to speak, but you also must listen. While listening, you must be in a posture of surrender. Surrendering is the process of giving up all you know to receive all of which you don't know, dismissing your reality for His truth. This means that as you open your mouth to pray, allow the pureness of your heart to utter out. This place often gets confused with babbling, just saying things with no direction. However, when we are in a boat that's drifting, we normally don't have direction. The fear of being lost with no insight into how to get back is worrisome and uneasy. That's why we must form a relationship that will teach us to listen as we speak so that our prayers may find direction from the spirit.

Surrendering to His direction will lead us back to our place of purpose. This is simply applying the instructions that He imparted in us to our "now" situation, instead of finding ways that make better sense from our understanding. It is not our job to find our own route. Faith requires fully and intentionally applying His instructions.

To "simply apply" sounds easy, but honestly, this is one of the most challenging parts. The pressure of feeling alone will cause you to pray. The prayer will cause you to listen for a response, but due to the temporary relief of response, choosing to "apply instructions" always seems tough.

Prayer may not be easy for everyone;

however, it is healthy and very much beneficial for anyone. The challenge of trying to be understood or trying to understand a foreign language is hectic. Due to the misunderstanding and confusion in communication, at times, we find ourselves looking for a much easier way out.

Instead of exercising the new language or putting in the work to learn this form of conversing, we find ourselves reasoning and substituting what we need for what we want.

An example of this looks like dismissing prayer for friendly advice, then dismissing our boldest thoughts for what may have sounded good at the moment. We essentially end up losing more and more of the original intake due to the lack of prayer. This is how the drift normally begins.

Leading me right to the depth of why the tool of prayer is vital. At some point in life, we experience a deep urge or calling. Some may receive intense visions or purposed signs that give us an idea of our destination. Whether it is something new—meaning we have never seen or experienced before—or it's something that we have been seeing for quite some time and have always had a deep feeling about. However we get to the vision, we must seek the One who is providing the provision.

It is so easy to get sidetracked and communicate with the wrong source. Most times, these experiences or urges get us all giddy and ready to share such news. There are other times when we get so excited about what we've heard or seen that we begin to move in our own might, which can cause us to catch that boat of drift. This is another place where we are found guilty of substitution. We find ourselves in a lack of patience, dismissing what is needed for what is wanted.

People will look at your life and see such light that God has placed in you and begin to push you in the direction of what they believe instead of in who they believe. **Warning!** Do not be tricked by the ways of PRAYERLESS people. They will direct you to places that they are familiar with instead of directing you to the source of your truth.

Conveying with them can be dangerous, for they forsake a sense of direction. Those that lead without direction expose their lack of impartation. We must be mindful to take all that we have and pray that God will reveal our truth and provide clarity and provision.

As you see here, communication with the right source is important. We must pray without ceasing. Pray about all things, no matter how big or small. The answers, or the directions, to the solution will always be found in prayer. It is in prayer that clarity is discovered. In order to overcome HER, clarity of who she is will need to be revealed.

Understand that the mind is a playground for the thought caster. The enemy takes pride in losing thoughts that he believes will kill steal and destroy you completely. With so many being cast the mind will quickly become cloudy, making it hard to decern what's true from what's false. Millions and millions of thoughts are being sent daily. Some are old, some are new, and some are just a repeat of a false reality that we have crossed paths with somewhere in life. When we find ourselves feeding into, or entertaining our thoughts, they become reality. Therefore, we desperately need clarity. Not all thoughts are good or positive. When we move on to the wrong pattern of thoughts, we lose coherence, soundness, good sense of who we are.

Prayer is the main tool to use when we are in a battle fighting for our pure identity, waring to conquer(her). Understand that prayer isn't just a "tool bag tool", but it's a weapon with much force. When we communicate with God, the words we use begin to saturate the land and manifest. We are opening our hearts and using our mouths to release power into the open space. When this culture of prayer is aligned with the will of God, nothing can stand in its way. It's like having a sealed and stamped check from the government with your name on it. The banks know to cash that check because it's aligned with the one who has enough power to shut them down. Surely, the funds will be available because they came from the place that created the funds.

Likewise, prayer with correct intentions has the FULL power to level mountains. How? Because they are the sealed and stamped check from the one who holds all power. The currency of prayer is never-ending when it's connected to the one who creates the coin.

Prayer provides insight. We go through many seasons in life: cold, hot, and in-between or, as many say, "the good, the bad, and the ugly". We experience things that are too challenging for our own understanding. Without prayer, we spend a life's worth of time trying to figure out why. This is that place where we are normally crying out in distress, singing, *Why me, and what did I do to deserve this?* Our eyes get cloudy, and most times, our ears are clogged. We can't see further than what happened when something is happening. We cannot afford to neglect the intimacy of prayer during such a time frame. We stand the chance to lose understanding of "HER", unconsciously allowing her to slip away.

One of the most precious moments is when we surrender in prayer with all our hurt and confusion, looking for understanding and guidance. This moment is beautiful because God doesn't turn us away or leave us in the dark. Instead, He provides insight. For some of us, it takes quite some time to understand His doing, but one thing is for sure: He's always strategic and purposeful. Meaning, He will, at times, allow things to happen that make no sense to us. All to find out later down the road that if we had not been through or gone through, the very thing that didn't make sense would not equate in purpose.

Prayer is fulfilling. Whatever becomes full can become empty. Throughout this journey, we will experience the pleasures of fullness. Joy will overtake us, and we will begin moving passionately toward our purpose. However, just as a car loses gas when it is used, so will we. Don't lose sight of yourself. Some people fill up their gas tank before it reaches the halfway mark, some fill up when they enter the red zone, and others ride on 'E' until the car is about to give in. Be wise and take good care of what belongs to you. Don't be the one burnt out each week because you didn't prioritize your gas. Spend your money wisely so that you can afford to ride out.

What am I saying? Through prayer, we gain the strength to carry on, but we need to be intentional while praying. We must pray for the things that concern the heart, but it's just as important that we pray for the concerned heart. Pray for "HER."

In prayer, we find the fulfillment of the things that we began to run low on—confidence, peace, compassion, joy, love, and anything that we share with others that help them along the way. Talking to God about these areas is a sure sign of trust, which is something we need when trying to conquer her. We don't normally speak about these vulnerable places due to the silent pain and or defense mechanism that we have gained. However, God fills these areas time and time again through prayer. Always remember that people can only fill voids temporarily, but God can and will fulfill any void that lacks attention permanently.

Use this tool to build a lifestyle of prayer. Let us not pray only when things are going bad but let us keep a communication line open for all things. When times are good, and life seems to be pleasing, may we worship God with our whole hearts in the same manner that we would if everything were falling apart? This tool of prayer will help us overtake everything that we come across, even when that thing is us.

We are, at times, our worse enemy. We seem to think we always know what's best for us, when without God the creator, we don't even understand how we work.

It makes me think about getting a new phone. I love that the creators made an app called tips that send you a message from time to time, inviting you to discover different things that your phone can do. If any of you are like me, most of the tips that they send, I would have never known the phone could do such a task without the help of the creator. I would have gone my entire life not knowing. I may have even gone as far as saying that they should create something that they already had created.

In the building of prayer, we have access to all our gifts and talents. Some things we have never tapped into, not because of our age or its just simply not time yet, but more so because we have no idea how they work or that we are even capable of doing them.

I encourage you to seek out all your tips and ask God in prayer how you are designed to work in this space that He has graced you in.

Prayers don't come with expiration dates; we should never stop applying pressure until we see the results of our prayer. Many of us love to lean on the phrase " I won't let go until you change my name." which comes from a story of someone clinging unto God fully until God moved on his need. Likewise, we are to keep praying and trusting until God responds to our needs and begins to move on them.

When we desire something desperately in life, we allow nothing to keep us from it. We call everyone we trust, looking for help to get what we desire. We stay up all hours of the day researching, and "looking for our yes," as we call it in church. We'll even seek a loophole. We don't let go; we don't stop applying pressure until something has moved or is changed. 'No' is never the end; we keep going till we get what we want.

> **Take note**: in order to conquer her, you CAN'T LET GO!

Life without prayer is a dangerous life. You may not notice the red flags right away, but surely, they are there. I equate it to the understanding of the human body. If we don't act to the needs of our body, we are putting ourselves in a danger zone, at risk of shutting down any day.

Some may relate to a vehicle better. If we never take time to care for our cars, their lifespan is shortened. They need gas often; the oil must be changed several times a year. Cleaning is a must; our attention must be tuned in to the car's needs often. We find that when we are not attentive in that area, things began to take a wrong turn, and trouble comes rushing in.

Life without prayer mirrors that image. When we are not in tune with God concerning all things, we become walking red flags. Without prayer, we will find ourselves leaning to our own understanding. Proverbs 3:5-6 states,

> *"Trust in the LORD with all your heart and lean not on your own understanding; in all ways submit to Him, and He will make your paths straight".*

So, we learn here that we can't journey this path alone it will be a complete war with ourselves. Trying to release anger and not holding grudges will overwhelm us. Stress will overtake us in areas that we should be able to freely be unbothered, and every tragedy outside our reach will have our name on it.

Prayer is our tool for release and increase. Flush out all the toxic waste that you've encountered during the boundless times of your life. Take hold of your inheritance of freedom and abundance. In prayer, we gain most of our riches and clear our debt. It can't be replaced with anything because it's our key to everything. Prayer should be our start and our finish.

Every day is a new day, one that has never been seen before. There will always be a need for insight into the unknown and understanding on our way through. We will never know the way without the Way-maker, and we can only get to Him through prayer.

Set time apart to meet with the Father. Don't commit to something that you can't do. Allow your prayer life to have room to grow and expand. Just as in friendships and relationships, the more you reach out, the deeper the intimacy becomes, and the deeper the intimacy, the stronger the commitment.

This will become one of your favorite tools if you don't abuse and misuse it. Don't compare your tool of prayer to anyone else's. Understand that just like any tool in the world, some are old, some are new, some are fancy, and some are plain, but one thing in common is that they all get the job done! It's according to individuals' preferences in how they are bought, but at the end of the day, if the tool is worked, it will work.

If you desire a newer model, there's nothing wrong with that. In time we all desire an upgrade. My only advice is that you work for it. We tend to appreciate things more when we invest in them ourselves. Trying to mimic someone's prayer life that they have mastered will only hinder you in the long run. Understand that they got where they got by exercising their prayers and continuously taking time to speak with the father on behalf of their heart.

That exercise is available to anyone who desires it. Our prayer life can speak things into existence to level mountains to heal, intercede on behalf of the brokenhearted to reach people in a completely different country, and most precious to build oneself up. Our prayer life is limitless. Whatever we speak can manifest.

Our words hold much power. That is why we must be very careful and intentional about what we speak. Praying is one of the greatest advantages we can use here on earth. Our words shoot out our mouths like seeds being planted into very fertile grounds. As we speak, there are assigned angels that begin to move as if they are watering the very seeds that we just planted. In due time those seeds will grow to allow the manifestation of what we spoke to form into existence.

Never forsake the tool of prayer. Again, I say the tool of prayer is a very vital tool. The first step to Conquering her is taking a step in prayer.

## TWO
# TOOL OF FAITH

What is Faith? Faith is the confidence in what we hope for and assurance about what we do not see, according to Hebrews 11:11. Faith is the action that we move in when we truly believe in what we're cheering for. It's knowing that as we push toward the goal, we are heading toward the fulfillment of what has yet to be seen with the naked eye.

Imagine speaking your victories into existence. In the fight world, you will come across a handful of determined champions. If you take time to watch their journey, you will find that many of them speak their fulfillment into actuality. They carry out a form of faith. Waking up each day, looking at themselves in the mirror and repeating the same ole song, *"I'm the greatest in the world, I can't be beat. I am the champion..."*. As they speak these powerful words into the atmosphere they proceed with an action. Day in and day out training to be the very thing they sing. When faith meets works the evidence is birthed.

Faith is the tool that brings revelation to our words. Proverbs 18:21 teaches,

> *"The tongue has the power of life and death, and those who love it will eat its fruit."*

Have you noticed that much of what you experience started from a seed planted by a WORD? When a word is planted inside of you, soon it will begin to grow. There's no favoritism in whether it's a good word or a bad word. When the seed is watered, it will grow. Meaning those words or thoughts that we allow to take residence in our mind will one day come to full existence.

We can't help but act out what we think about. In one way or another, it exposes itself in the flesh. That's why many say people can tell their truth by their facial expressions and or body language. In many cases, when we have a desire, we begin to work for it or towards it. You can tell a person's true desire by the way they apply pressure in that area.

Faith is the key that opens every promised door and levels every rocky mountain. A door is used to enter, exit, welcome, and keep things out. In order to obtain our desires, we must get through the obvious opposition by faith.

Speaking a thing to be so—without reaching for the spoken word— breaths fairy tale into the atmosphere. It shows that you are a vessel of weak faith. Maybe you've experienced faith before but never understood it. Believe what you say and say what you believe. Let your faith be strong.

We control the action of what we do, not the movement of what faith does. Although it is based on the way we proceed as we carry out the intentions of what we speak, it is God that will release the plenitude of what's to come.

Say it, then do it. Faith applies pressure to fear, causing it to bow down to the authority that's held within. If you're getting chased by a dog, fear is bold. The action of its truth is manifesting as you continue to move in it. With that same knowing, that if the dog can't catch you then he can't harm you. You run from a dog with great hope that you'll get away. Though you haven't quite seen the full escape, you move quickly to partake in its fullness. When we operate like this in our everyday lives, we begin to see more and more of the desires of our hearts fulfilled and the plan that will prosper us revealed.

Jeremiah 29:11 says,

*For I know that plans that I have for you, declares the Lord, plans that will prosper you and not harm you...*

Apart from faith, we dwell in fear. Like oil and water, the two won't mix. They are a true danger to one another. Fear keeps us from God's prosperous plans. Fear is designed to hurt us by crippling our authority to call things as they are. Faith breaks the rules of fear, building testimonies of unshakable truths.

Many times, it is challenging to speak to things that are greater felt than seen. The tool of faith is beneficial in this area of need. An example of this is found in the lives of those who choose God's plan over reality. Sometimes reality says sickness is on you and because you're wearing it belongs to you. God's plan says sickness isn't your portion, pick up your faith and walk healed. Fear will tag team with reality and try to mentally destroy you while Faith will tag team with God and perform a miracle.

The tool of faith brings things to existence that the world already calls dead. Impossibilities are now possible, creating the distinction between spoken words and the ability to live by the spirit. Although there is much to grasp at the root of faith let's get into some of the *"faith tips"*.

Faith requires patience, demands trust, but without work, it is dead. As you see, this tool is a package with three helpful accessories: patience, trust, and work.

To be confident is to feel sure, and to feel sure is to be convinced. In order to activate this tool, you must be willing to apply effort and get rid of the empty profession. Saying things with a lack of knowledge and God's wisdom.

What does it look like to apply effort and get rid of an empty profession concerning the tool of faith? In its simplest example, it's living out loud in the words you speak. *"Don't just say it, do it!"* There's an old saying that says, *"Faith it 'til you make it"*. Allow the life of your words to flow. What you speak should always be in the work of coming to the past.

I can say, "I'll be a millionaire by this time next year" all year long; however, if I do nothing but sleep and eat all day and then repeat the same ole song day in and day out, my words will literally be nothing but a sad, depressing song.

Some things never inherit their rightful gain simply because when we speak of them, we barely believe what we said ourselves. Some things get a spark of life and die out before it reaches their full potential because we abandon the faith to adopt doubt. Faith and doubt are enemies of one another. You can't be friends with both. Where faith is meant to live doubt is sent to kill.

**Take note:** Certain tools come with extra accessories.

One tool is the drill. Many drills come with special additional pieces called bits. These bits come in many shapes and sizes to change in and out depending on how big or small the job is.

Something I've noticed from using numerous tools, especially those that are in the same category as the drill, is that you must be ready to put some work in, applying pressure at the appropriate time. Although the drill may be what's needed to get the job done, it doesn't mean that without the proper force, it will fulfill the need.

I like to look at faith as one of the tools that depend upon extra accessories. There are times we only need the original tool in order to reach our right now needs. I like to believe those are the times when we insert a mustard seed of faith. However, there are other needs that will cause us to use the accessories connected to the tool.

Patience, trust, and works are three of the main accessories that faith requires. *Conquering (HER)* is a journey, and it can take quite some time with much work involved. Therefore, patience and trust are needed. Times will get difficult, and change will seem nonexistent. Nevertheless, it is faith that will keep you on the path of overcoming her.

The tool of faith allows us to reach past all that we see with the natural eye and put a surpassing belief in all that we need in the spiritual realm. This need isn't one that lives in the grey areas of wishful wants, but it dwells in the brighter areas of our purpose. If we truly desire to *conquer her*, we must look past our natural ability and seek out the abilities of God.

The comfort in doing only what we believe we can do has an expiration date. When we find ourselves still trying to thrive in our own abilities past that expiration date, we become irritable. Be encouraged to use that uncomfortably to seek out the abilities of God.

He can do all things, even those that we look to be impossible due to our current or past lack of qualifications. Keep this truth in your heart. The expectation of the world's qualifications bows to the qualifications of God every time. Meaning, what you need in order to qualify for certain things in the world is not relevant to what you may need to approve for the promises of God.

Romans 8:30 lets us know that He predestined us, He called us, He justified us, and glorified us. This is an encouraging scripture; however, it takes much faith to walk into such truth.

We must believe with our whole hearts that before we were even born, He had a plan for us.

He knew of all the mistakes we would make, and He prepared a way to clean them up. This can be a challenge to trust when we are filled with only knowledge of the world, meaning no spiritual impartation and revelation of our identity.

Being world bound sometimes blinds us from spiritual fullness. That's why it is so vital to follow the principles in the Bible that were left behind. These principles will lead us to a lifestyle of obedience which will help us in our faith. Let's look at how they work together.

Faith summons obedience, ordering us to abide in the work of what was spoken. Whenever a person has the power of authority to summons someone, that *"someone"* is required to come. If for whatever reason that *"someone"* doesn't respond, there is an account to be held.

By the same token, when we do not demonstrate active faith our goals, dreams, visions, jobs, finical increases, spiritual growth, or whatever the promise intel will be on hold and sometimes even passed down to the next in line. It is mind-blowing to witness the doors that open for us when we are actively responding to our faith, yet it is devastating to testify what you knew deep down on the inside of you be rewarded to someone else due to their obedience.

Did you know that it's impossible to please

God without faith? We are to find ourselves drawing close to Him as He draws near to us. Without trusting in Him it's as if we're betting against Him. When we are putting our trust in others we are pulling away from God. With that same truth, if we can't please God, how can we expect the attachment of a family curse, the distractions from our adversaries, mental death, evil illnesses and sickness, or years of bondage to be broken. Without fully submitting and working the plan of the one who takes charge we are making a bold statement that connects with fear rather faith.

The tool of faith holds a power of its own. This power is one that can cause the storms of life to become settled right before our eyes. When I was much younger, I would say, "I wish I had the power to become invisible." I thought that was one of the coolest powers in the world. You could be standing right next to someone, and they wouldn't even know it.

As life went on, I never knew that the access to become invisible was always within reach. As I grew in my belief in God, I noticed that my faith began to stretch, and as my faith stretched, the troubles of life began to feel as if they were able to stand right next to me, but many times never touch me. I was, in a sense, INVISIBLE.

We should practice giving faith permission to our actions. The more permission you allow faith to have in your life, the more you will begin to unlock all its possibilities. Faith isn't just a cool word. It's a word packed with action, ready to produce over and over again.

As we exercise faith we will find the necessity of patience. Patience is a peaceful call to wait while faith is demanding movement. Patience will allow you to rest at ease in your work while believing that what you are doing is causing something to form.

You see, while some things will form in the moment, others will form overnight, and then there are those great quantities of fulfillments that will occur in the future. No matter the wait, we must never lose hope. In order to stay connected, we must have patience.

During this process, anxiousness will try its best to creep in, but remember not to be anxious, instead, pray about everything. It is our job to make sure we keep our minds covered, banishing every thought that goes against our beliefs. You may feel more familiar with this when it's labeled as doubt. Hesitation is sent from the enemy, leaving us to be uncertain about what we spoke about. It's his way of killing the seed that was meant to live, remember, his job is always to kill steal and destroy. So, anything that you can identify one or all three of these red flag bearers in your life know that it is apart from your purpose.

When we find ourselves being anxious and doubtful, we are that much closer to losing our grip on patience. During this type of emergency, we must grab hold of our tool of prayer and speak patience back over our situation. Pray God's word in the midst of your storm and look for the storm to clam. Patience is going to help us along the way, never giving up on the very thing that we have been charging our faith in.

Using our accessory of trust, with our tool of faith, is what determines how big of a job we can do.

Little trust equates to little faith. Much trust equates to much faith. If I trust that God will allow me to see tomorrow in faith, I will begin to plan my day. If I have no trust that I will see next week due to sickness, in fear, I will begin saying my goodbyes. However, if I trust God to be my healer, then no matter the sickness, in faith, I will continue to move forward. I will find patience in my healing, believing that one day soon I will be complete in my body. Little trust produces little faith, while much trust produces big faith.

Trust expresses the volume of our truth. You can tell how truthful someone is about a situation if you watch their action of trust. Certainty is only clear when we put our faith in God. Moving in the boldness of His command.

Trust echo's the most inner depths of our faith. How easy is it to say with our mouth that we stand on whatever God says is best for our life, but then prepare for what we believe is best for our life? This is called an empty profession. In this case, the trust that we shout about is nothing more than a broken vow. Trust needs understanding, which is best recognized as fully submitting repeatedly—no mater if we gain from it or lose from it.

When I was in one of the darkest places of my life, everything around me went against everything that I was purposed to be. Every so often, I would remember that greatness was my destiny. At that moment, I would speak broken promises to myself, hoping God would lead me into the light so that I could see the path of which I was supposed to take.

I thought I was exercising faith by just believing that I would one day come out of that place. I tell you the truth, It wasn't until the moment that I began to work my faith that things started moving towards the light. I worked my faith by putting my words to action. Trusting that what I was doing was investing in my next.

I had to get to a vulnerable place allowing myself to understanding that it took time to get me to the place that I was in, so it may take time to get me out. Emotions were hard to keep under control, but with the help of prayer, I found patience to be useful.

There were many times that I wanted to slip back into everything that I worked to break away from, but thanks be to God that as I worked my faith, He worked His power to provide escape after escape. I continually surrendered to His plan, and the manifestation of what I was looking for did not only become my current, but it was much better than I could have ever imagined it to be.

**Take note:** Faith is an action that must be

worked on daily. All you need is a mustard seed of faith to level a mountain. If there is a mountain between you and your destiny, work the little faith that you have till it becomes strong enough to conquer her.

# THREE
# TOOL OF CONSISTENCY & DISCIPLINE

These are what I like to call "much needed bonus tools." They work together yet are very powerful alone. It's best that they are used together. One without the other can cause a stressful disaster in the long run. Believe me. I've been there and done that.

Consistency has the will to build the building, but discipline has the tendency to keep the building. What good is a building that can't stand? Not all architects are great at building. It takes a wise constructor to keep together what was put together. You'll find in the art of building that it's not a one-man-job. Not saying that one can't build alone, but stating that one alone won't stand.

In just about anything that we set out to accomplish, it will call for the need for consistency. The more we work on the plan, the closer we get to the goal. Consistency has a powerful drive that enforces such results. However, just like most things' consistency has a weakness too. Consistency can easily turn into fruitless habits. A tree that bears no fruit is unproductive and vain.

Meaning, that we can take our good work habits and forget the purpose behind them, which will cause us to lose our drive. Just like working out, when we lose track of what we are aiming for, we lose track of making sure we keep the same quality. More reps with less quality equate to pointless results. This is how we, more times than less, fall back into that deep trap of feeling as though we just can't be helped. As the idiom goes, "You're darned if you do; darned if you don't."

I've made that comment several times on this journey. It wasn't until I learned to use discipline with consistency that I found myself dismissing that saying. Being careful not to favor one over the other, but more so balancing both to the best of my ability.

This may look like fewer reps but steady quality, so in the long run, we reap better results. The more we practice the principle, the greater we reap in quantity.

We get so caught up in comparison that that we look past what should be great to settle for temporary achievement. Remember this: *the promise is meant to last.* Settlement isn't designed to conquer. I consider these tools *consistency and discipline* a must-have because without them, we could never fully overcome *"her"*.

Although she will forever be a work in progress, we must understand that during the course, piece by piece, she will need gratification and a stem of fruitful enrichment. Both can be found in the balance of these tools.

Consistency is going to make sure that you keep fighting. See how energetic it is? This is the push that's very much needed. If we only fight for one or two rounds and the depth of what we are fighting against still has a fight in it, then we have fought a pointless fight. Therefore, consistency alone will become weak and defeated. Now what good is that?

Discipline is consistency's best friend when attuned to the force behind the push. With the two joined, they become a more impactful tool. This reminds me of the power of *two or more gathered in Jesus' name*. God puts His stamp of approval on the things that they united about.

Discipline will remind consistency of the *"why"*. Why we started, why it's necessary, why we need to keep going, and so on. Discipline will help her see results along the way, results that will carry her through the tougher seasons. To *overcome her*, she will need much discipline. Discipline to withstand every battle it takes to pull her through. Consistency —although is the start—is the balance between the two that will subdue her.

Many of us have grown to exercise one and suffer from the lack of the other. How many times has it felt as if you had it all together, the push was right, the force was strong, yet somewhere down the line, you gave in and didn't reach the success of conquering?

This is bold in so many areas of our life. It's time to change the outcome of this ongoing battle. It's time to take back what belongs to you and *conquer her.*

Recognizing the need for help and understanding that something must be done in order to get her back on the right track is only the start. This is a challenging state because most times, we start but lack the tools to finish the job. Being consistent is the start adding discipline guarantees completion.

When I was at the beginning of maturing my walk of faith, there was something crying out from the inside of me that needed help. Change was determined to find me, but I continuously chose to sit in the comfort of my hiding place. I wasn't ready to receive the unknown. After all, I knew exactly what it looked like to be where I was and what to expect when things didn't go in the right direction. The challenge of trying to figure out how things would be if I moved according to the cry would seem so overwhelming at times.

Every so often, I would find myself answering the cry, and afterward, I felt so good but that was only momentarily. I will carry on, journeying throughout life until the impulse would occur again. I grew to learn that something needed to change, and I needed to identify it quickly. I learned to place myself in a position that would stop leading me back to the same ole drought, the place that left the inside of me empty.

This was when I made the decision to

consistently nourish the void. I thought with consistency, surely, I wouldn't fall back into that empty place. So, I did everything that I could believing that this change would become my new place of comfort. Little did I know that this trip of consistency would soon become a habitual lifestyle that still suffered a lack.

I got so tangled in filling the void that I lost focus on why I was filling the void. I forgot about the place that used to cry out in emptiness. I lost track of the connection that would draw me back to the things that were purposed to fill the void. My *"why"* was nowhere to be found. At this point, I was just living, doing all that I could while producing fruitless habits.

Soon I found myself unraveling, spiraling backward, lost, not understanding why or where it even began. I started thinking that life was so much better in my old place of comfort. The more I dwelled on these thoughts, the closer I found myself attracted to the roots of my old habits. However, this time there was a difference; something changed. Now that I have experienced what it was like to continuously fill my voids with positive and purposed insight, I knew that I couldn't stay in that weak place. So, I got up from that position, strength was gained from consistency. This time as I proceeded, I went in with a new plan. Consistency gained a friend named discipline, and together working with both, balancing the two, I was able to *conquer her.*

# FOUR
# TOOL OF FORGIVENESS

Forgiveness is her way to freedom. The usage of this tool is normally rare but produces great results. Forgiveness has the authority to release not only the one who is receiving it

but the one who is offering it as well. This tool extends the life of her far more than you can imagine. Unforgiveness is one of the heaviest weights to carry, and anything that has to carry weight if not carried properly will cut back its life span drastically.

Have you ever found yourself rooted in bitterness due to a past situation that you never received an honest apology from? Every time you find yourself talking about the situation, this peak of negativity slips right through your lips before you can catch it. When someone else mentions anything that almost sounds like that sour patch you experienced, your body language can't help but respond even if your words don't.

That's because the command that's connected to forgiveness hasn't been released in that area of your life. This is damaging to your spirit and your mental state. Forgiveness will destroy the roots of that bitter place and add life to the lack of that which was shortened. When we forgive it orders the suffering and discomfort to leave and give room for restoration to take place.

Becoming comfortable in discomfort is a norm, sadly we are taught to bear it then to rid it. This life lesson was born through the heart of wounded people and its far from God's truth. God desires us to live in a liberty and anything that is overbearing He instructs us to give to Him that He may bear it. *Matthew 11:28 Come to me all you who are weary and burdened, and I will give you rest.*

The tool of forgiveness heals areas that can't always be seen by the natural eye. It releases the pressure that's weighing down the heart. It will ease the mind during restless seasons and will silence the chaos in your heart. What's in your heart will soon consume you, this is why it's important that forgiveness is found providing you room to understand and let go.

Forgiveness operates on the deepest cuts and peals back the toughest layers, preparing room for the fulness of relief that many of us lack. When it's used in its proper function, forgiveness sets the atmosphere for love and welcomes wholeness with open arms. We rarely acknowledge the many layers packed on when we are stern in not yielding to compassion.

What is the appropriate role of forgiveness? We are to make a conscious decision to let free of resentment towards them they and those who hurt you whether its deserved or not. It's never easy because our true emotions are involved, however its necessary.

Many times, we find ourselves struggling to love the one that selfishly grips our due forgiveness. One way or another, we connect the lack of forgiveness with disrespect, and once the respect is lost, we struggle to extend love. We can't conquer her if we don't respect her. She's attracted to love. It's her deity.

Understand that forgiveness isn't only a tool that you have to lend out often, but it's also a tool that can be adjusted for you to use for yourself. Get in a place where you can confront all your wrongdoing, your mess- ups and disappointment, empty your safe, leaving nothing behind. Don't allow this challenge to overtake you due to miss guidance. Most of us grew up under the teaching that those errors in life are things you take to your grave. If you aren't careful those errors in life are the very things that will bring you to your grave.

Your life depends on the freedom that you owe it. Taking regret to the grave looks like a life of silent misery. Past failure is hunting you at random peeks of your life. This is not your promised end. Forgive her! Choose what God has for you and not what the pain of others offers you.

Listen clearly, Past secrets don't belong in your safe zone. We should desire to leave this place empty, giving everything, we have, be free from everything that claimed us under a false identity and live in peace. Holding on to the past gets heavy, and it takes up room that the future needs.

We are to forgive as the Lord forgives. Let go and pursue life as if it never happened. Casting out all regret and embarrassment.

*Conquer her* by forgiving her! She deserves it. May her past be her past and her future be her purpose.

In the same way that a new relationship opportunity presents itself when one forgives another, so does oneself open that door to a new relationship when she forgives self. Learn to let go and live unchained. Her purpose isn't built on her past. It was prearranged, awaiting her willingness to follow suit, let go and grow.

We have been trained to forgive but not forget, and honestly, I used to hate hearing that until I took a different look at it. The idea of how it's taught is to remember what was done, all while holding a silent mental grudge that safely keeps a seed of bitterness. This is not good for the heart; therefore, there's a lack of pure freedom.

We should desire to forgive without any strings attached, meaning completely erasing the mistake that was made without holding mental tally marks. Sometimes forgetting can cause a lack of growth when not done properly. We are not called to be ignorant, allowing habits of what was done in error to repeat themselves comfortably without making wise choices to prevent it.

However, we should use that opportunity to fuel her when in need of encouragement on how far she's grown. Always hoping for the better while understanding that flaws are active. Gaining wisdom in the midst while preparing to forgive again, as we are caught in our flaws, this is what we expect others to do. As high as our expectations are when we are standing in error, hoping to be fully forgiven, we should put this into practice with ourselves.

As I began to grow more into my identity, I began to gain an impeccable understanding of forgiveness. My actions proved that I *conquered her* through forgiveness, forgiving her for everything she was found guilty of, meaning holding her to no accounts of past wrongdoing. But grasp this, I've learned that I truly never forgot and that taught me that forgiving without forgetting is not always a bad thing.

*Conquering her* is a beautiful thing to see. Sometimes you must take a glance at where it all started to comprehend where it's going. Forgiveness taps into that place of love where it holds no account of wrongdoing. When we forgive, it shows love because it doesn't delight in the evil which lives in the house of its opposite. It unlocks patience, which mirrors love. It takes forgiving her to unlock loving her.

Forgetting leaves room for the same error to occur again, "holding no accounts". Remember to use wisdom so that you are not overtaken by practiced errors. Forgetting also opens the door for lies to grow and for the truth to be rejected, yet it also reintroduces trust and sets the tone for growth, use decrement to navigate through such field.

You see, to produce the pure action of forgiveness, we must learn how to use the tool gracefully. This will teach

us how to wholeheartedly forgive without forgetting while forgiving as forgetting.

Ask yourself this "are you willing to put everything aside to *conquer her*"? Holding on to things is what I like to call an unseen aggravating comfort. You can't quite see the thing that's causing you to behave in those frustrating behaviors. However, you have a good idea of what or where it is coming from. You choose to leave the situation at bay because you feel like it's more comfortable to keep it instead of uprooting it. Are you willing to put everything aside and deal with the root of her, or will you rather remain uncomfortably comfortable?

Forgiveness releases the pain while overthrowing the roots of failure, disappointment, and shame. Whenever forgiveness is about to be released, it feels as if everything around you gets extremely tight. It's as if the air is sucked out of the atmosphere. The things that you are deeply rooted in begin to entangle themselves tighter than they have ever been before.

Therefore, most times, we would rather relax in that aggravating comfort of our mistakes than deal with the pressure that comes before the release.

Have you ever had to apologize to someone knowing that they were wrong and you were right? Do you remember that feeling that went before you? That is the most aggravating pressure. You must push past every single bit of pride and tackle that situation at full speed.

She awaits to be forgiven. To *conquer her*, you must forgive her!

# FIVE
# TOOL OF LOVE

The tool of love is a very special tool, It's honestly one of my favorites. The weight of love is unmeasurable, and that's what makes it set apart. In all the years that I've been graced to see, I noticed that pure love is unmatched and unprecedented. It proceeds to do things that go against the grain. Deeper than street love, tougher than brotherly love, and proven to be unconditional.

I've struggled so much in life due to choosing the *"love"* of the world and all of its pleasures, that I blatantly had a hard time grasping what it means to really love. Many people can't tap into the fullness of love being absolute, whole, and life-filling, simply because of the illusion of worldly love misunderstood to be godly love.

The world projects that love hurts and that it is okay to dabble in and out of it. You can love someone one day and hate them the next. We have lost sight of the pureness of love by allowing God to be absent from our everyday lives. We are surly flawed, but He still loves us. We would recognize this if we made room for him and our busy schedules. When we learn the way that he loves us it will cause us to mirror that into the world however when we obtain the way the world loves us and that same manner we mirror that to those we are connected to.

The tool of love is your most valuable tool. All the tools have an important area where they are to be used, but love is the top tool that fits in all areas. It is the handy Mandy tool that ultimately gets the job done.

God gave us the perfect example of love when he gave us his one and only son, Jesus, so that anyone who believes in him will have eternal life.

This teaches us that love is a tool that must be given. It has no benefit just sitting in the bag. Having it and giving it are two different sayings. To have love, pure love is to have the spirit of Jesus dwell with you for He is the essence of love. To give love is to share His ways and not those of the world. This is how it covers all.

I truly believe if you have it, you will give it. Love isn't crafted to be tucked away. It's always to be in use.

God knew that we needed the ultimate sacrifice in order to even stand a chance for life in the Kingdom. He knew that we were going to be in so many horrific conditions that there would be no way for us alone to find our way back home. So, he gave through the example of love to redeem us.

There's a realm of the Kingdom here that we are welcome to take part in, the Kingdom of God. We can't enjoy this beautiful opportunity if we don't exercise our tool of love. Love will open the door to the Kingdom of God and grant us access to live abundantly.

We have found so many ways to allow tainted versions of love to enter our hearts that we miss the opportunities to thrive in pure love. Through love, she can be healed from all the broken mistakes. The thoughts in her mind that hold her hostage will have to let her go when it's approached by real love. Others may extend it, but until you offer it, she will be forever captive.

She'll remain in her room of guilt and shame. Even if you took the necessary steps to forgive her, without love, the battle would turn into a war. She will continue to feel enslaved to not being good enough.

People can wrap her in their arms, kiss her forehead, and refuse to let her go, but until you treat her with that same energy, she will live in seasons of worthless living.

Love the most important tool of them all. Love covers everything. It destroys the chaos, blinds the shame, and heals the pain. Love doesn't need anything attached to it. It's strong enough all by itself.

Are you willing to love her?

As the Bible tells us in 1 Corinthians, Love is patient

and kind. It does not envy nor boast. It is not proud. It doesn't dishonor others, and it's not self-seeking. It's not easily angered; it keeps no record of wrongs. Love does not delight in evil but rejoices with the truth. It always protects, always hopes, always persevere. Love never fails Love is what will fulfill her need. We can't rescue her without it. Every bit of texture that love has in it is necessary. It's packaged with the best ingredients from the originator himself. I believe, for that reason,

love never fails.

Looking back at all she's been through, the hectic journey that has led her to this place of misery, true comfort is what she lacks. Those around her have lost patience for her, leaving you to be her last result.

She's judged through flawed eyes and misunderstood by close friends, which has created an atmosphere where kindness can't be found. Fake smiles are forced, and aggressive attitudes rise as she's silently seeking to be loved and feel a sense of acceptance.

Love fills the void of all she lacks. It sends the hope she cries out for. Love is packed with so much healing that it's nearly impossible for her to remain the same.

Our past is simply "just that," the past. Although it might try to shape our future, it can only have access to what we allow. In life, we will cross paths with various moments of experiencing hardships. Some of these challenges will be a lot harder than others. It's all about how we handle the hardship and how much authority we give over to hardship.

We can either allow it to get the best of us or get the best of it. The sad part is most of us don't understand how much control we have over the hardship until we come out of it.

The moment we choose ourselves over the issues we've encountered, we become one step closer to the love we are called to. The love that's patient, the love that hopes and always perseveres.

Choosing yourself invites patience to the mistakes. It grasps the understanding that a healthy mental state outweighs stress and disappointment. But my favorite part is that it perseveres in forgiveness.

As she begins to grow out of the place of defeat, she will need much love. More times than often, she will look back on the mistakes she's made and feel regret. Love will be her answer. It will protect her from the past and direct her to her future.

When defeat was my place of residence, I honestly forgot my worth. In my eyes, my worth was all that was right in front of me, nothing. So, each day I proceeded with the lack of worth that I've seen. This kept me in a broken state for way too long.

When I finally began to journey out, I would experience moments of past regret, and it would try its best to drag me back. It was the grip of love that kept me moving forward. Never judging me for desiring to go back, never holding grudges with me because I wasn't fully recovered but always reminding me of where I was heading and who I was becoming. With love, there was no condemnation.

Love always saw the better side of me and encouraged me to get there. This isn't saying that it's easy. It's proving that it's possible. The love of the world won't do it, it's not strong enough, but the love of God that works through you has the strength to *conquer her*.

The greatest tool is love. It never declines. Take this moment to pray for her, have faith that your prayers are in action, working to pull her out of that dark place. Be consistent with the force of discipline so that she may not slip out of your hands. You can do this. Remember, forgiveness is key. Forgive without keeping tally's on how many times you've done this before and LOVE her out loud. My prayers are with you as you *CONQUER HER*!

# ABOUT THE AUTHOR

**Amanda Barr Herd**

Her name means, "worthy of love." And from the moment that she was born, she has exemplified the very essence of it. Amanda Barr Herd is a writer who teaches, inspires, motivates, and activates people to tap into the truth of what love is for themselves, for each other, and for God. A powerful woman of prayer, Amanda is known for the graceful way she leads others and the sound wisdom that she so effortlessly imparts into all that she meets.

Through many trials, tough times, and situations that have tried to take her out, Amanda has conquered and continued to win over and over again, leaning solely on her faith and her love for her family. She uses every lesson and tool that she has acquired while trying to navigate through this broken world as fuel to help her thrive and build a community of love and acceptance for those who need it the most.

Through her podcast CircleUp with Amanda Herd, you can learn how to love and be loved, acquiring every necessary tool to grow into the best version of yourself. Her Virtual Coffee meetups allow you to tell your story and hear the stories of others that will energize and revive you. Her business CircleUp Enterprise will help you birth, brand and grow your business to a place of success and triumph.

Amanda truly enjoys everything that she does and everything she touches bears witness through immaculate growth. She currently resides in Garner, NC with her husband Zac and their two kids Zakheus and Ariah.

*For booking, email circleup.ah@gmail.com*

Made in the USA
Columbia, SC
04 May 2023